PREPARING OUR DAUGHTERS
FOR
Puberty

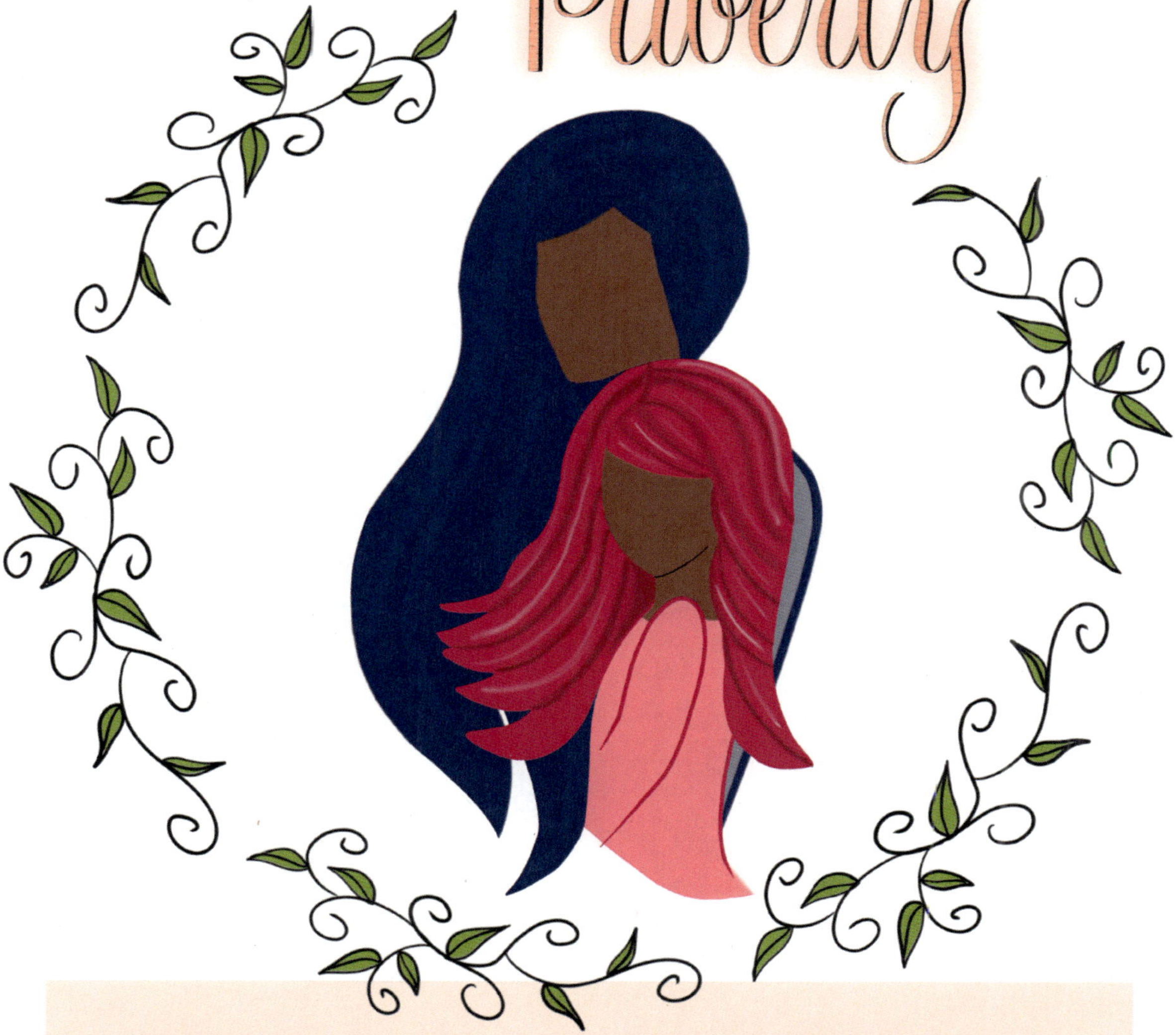

A MOTHER-DAUGHTER BIBLE STUDY

LUISA RODRIGUEZ

Preparing Our Daughters for Puberty

A Mother-Daughter Bible Study

For permissions contact: info@fruitfullywrite.com

ISBN 9798354028085

Book Design and Illustrations by Luisa Rodriguez

Fruitfully Write, LLC
PO Box 0417
Wasco, IL 60183-417
www.FruitfullyWrite.com

Contents

About the Author

Luisa Rodriguez is a military wife and a mom to two girls. She is the creator and writer of FruitfullyLiving.com, a website that helps women understand their God-given roles and purpose according to the scriptures. She is also the author of *A Royal Mission*, a Christian fairytale for young girls as well as the creator and designer of numerous notebooks and journals. Luisa advocates for young girls and women through her writing and illustrations.

Follow Luisa

Twitter: @FruitfullyLive
Facebook: @FruitfullyLiving
Instagram: @FruitfullyLiving

How to Use This Study

Remember the days when your little girl never worried about how her body looked? Sure, she loved to play dress-up, rummage through your jewelry and beg to wear make-up. She might have even asked you, "Mom, do I look pretty?" But she didn't worry about whether her nose was too big or if her waist was too wide. Those were the good ol' days!

Now the bodies of our little princesses will begin to change dramatically (if they have not already). They will become self-aware, and they may become uncomfortable in their own bodies. Social media, comments from their friends, schoolmates, and even movies and shows will begin to shape how they feel about themselves. And as mothers (and fathers), we must intentionally counteract it with God's word.

Not Meant to Be a Complete Biology Lesson

My intention behind this study is to help you introduce the concept of puberty to young girls while helping them develop a positive self-image. It is not intended to be an exhaustive discourse on all the biological changes that will occur during puberty, although we will discuss quite a few and we will introduce the reproductive organs and the formal names for body parts using illustrations as a guide.

Even though this study is not an exhaustive biology lesson, it is meant to spur questions and help your daughter feel comfortable talking about her changing body. I encourage you to use her curiosity to take the discussions from each lesson further and provide her with more information if she needs it.

How to Handle Chapter Six

Chapter six is an age-appropriate introduction to sex. Unfortunately, in the age of the internet, kids are getting exposed to sexual content at very young ages. For that reason, it is imperative that we, as Christian parents, beat the culture to the punch by introducing the concept from God's perspective. If you really feel your daughter is not ready for it, don't worry, just skip Lesson Six.

But if you are willing to give it a shot, here is my advice. Don't be weird about it. Our inclination is to be hesitant to talk about sex with our kids and it will show. This is the time to put on that poker face and not let your kids smell fear. If they sense that from you, they won't want to talk to you about it. Instead, they will go to their friends where they will get horrible advice and information. So, relax, be nonchalant about it and trust me, the questions will pour in!

Don't Just Give the Book to Your Daughters to Read!

I do not recommend that you just hand this book off to your girls as something for them to read. This book will spark a million questions and they need a safe place to talk about it all. They need you there to walk alongside them as they learn about their bodies.

What you can do, is read the book to them. I understand that some parents may have a hard time knowing what to say so I wanted to make it as easy as possible. But if you feel confident about the subject matter, then don't follow it word for word and just use it as a guide.

I do provide some questions in some of the lessons to help with engagement. Just remember to pause after the questions so the girls have time to answer!

Use Your Bibles!

This book has the Bible verses printed each time they are referenced. However, have your daughter use her Bible and encourage her to find and read the scriptures herself.

Have Materials Ready for the Craft

Finally, review the lesson beforehand for any materials you may need. Each lesson finishes off with a craft, and you will need to have supplies ready if you choose to incorporate the craft.

Now let's jump in together and help our girls understand why their bodies are changing! And just how amazing that can be!

Lesson 1: Created in His Image

Girls, did you know that you were created in the image of God? The Bible tells us so in the very first book of the Bible, Genesis. Let's read it together.

> So God created man in his [own] image, in the image of God created he him; male and female created he them.
>
> **Genesis 1:27 (ESV)**

We learn here that both boys and girls were created in God's image. Let's explore what that means.

An image is a physical representation of something else. Photographs, for example, are images of people and places. They are very accurate representations because they generally show every detail true to form (features, color). If you want to have an even more accurate image you might create a sculpture. Your image is no longer two-dimensional (flat), but three-dimensional (not flat).

We can take images in the opposite direction where they still represent something else but do not show every detail. Picasso is a famous artist whose images are not exact representations of his subjects. For example, a woman painted by Picasso might be made up of a series of squares and triangles with very vivid colors. Although we may not be able to see every finger or eyelash in a woman painted by Picasso, we can still tell that his painting represents a woman.

How do the drawings in Figure 1 represent the same woman but in different ways?

Figure 1

In the same way, God created us to represent Him. Our bodies may not be exact representations of God, but they were created, painted, and sculpted to represent Him. Why does that matter?

Let's go back to our friend Picasso. Even though his images are not exact representations, they are still worth a lot of money. How much? Each painting can sell for $4 million, $5 million, or even $6 million! Some would even say that his paintings are priceless!

Picasso's paintings are worth that much because he is an important artist.

Well, who is the most important artist of all? Who sculpted trees that sway? Who intricately painted beautiful patterns on a butterfly? Who masterfully created you?

GOD!!

If God, the most important artist of all, created you, how much do you think you are worth?

Well, it gets better than that. Remember Genesis 1:27 tells us that God not only created us but that He created us in His image! Whoa! Our bodies, our physical form, are an image of God. Not like a photograph that shows every detail because God is God, and we can never be like God. But think of it more like a Picasso.

Through broad strokes and imaginative colors, the masterpiece cannot fully represent the subject, but it is still priceless.

As we continue in our studies and talk more about our bodies and how they will be changing soon (if they have not already), remember just how much those precious bodies are worth!!

QUESTIONS for discussion:

1. How does it make you feel that God created you in His image?
2. Do you think God would ever make a mistake in the way that He created your body?
3. If God gave you a painting that He made, would you ever criticize it?
4. Based on what you learned in today's lesson, do you think that you should ever criticize your own body or anyone else's? Why or why not?

Craft: Self-Portraits

It is time to find the Picasso in you!! In today's craft, you will learn how some images can represent something exactly while others can illustrate a beautiful representation that is not exact. You will do so by drawing self-portraits, that is drawing pictures of yourself.

Tools:

Paper
Colored pencils, crayons, markers, or paints.

Directions:

Draw two self-portraits. The first self-portrait will be a picture that represents you accurately to the best of your ability. Then draw another one like a Picasso. Use my examples above to help you come up with some ideas.

Lesson 2: Woven and Knit Together

Last time we learned about being created in God's image. How wonderful was that? Today, we will look at how carefully God created each of us and why it matters.

Let's read Psalm 139:13-14

> [13] For you formed my inward parts; you knitted me together in my mother's womb. [14] I praise you, for I am fearfully and wonderfully made. Wonderful are your works; my soul knows it very well.
>
> **Psalm 139:13-14 (ESV)**

When you first became a life in your mama's womb (inside of her belly), you started off as a series of cells. If you haven't learned what a cell is yet, they look ike tiny blobs and gazillions of them make up a person. Your hand, your nose, your heart— are all made up of these itty, bitty cells.

In your mother's womb, your cells continued to replicate forming your heart, your lungs, your arms, and even your reproductive organs (more on what these are later). This continued to happen for nine months until one glorious day your little body had everything it needed to live outside of your mother's womb, and you were born!

Ahh, but your body did not stop growing then. Outside of the womb, you grew bigger, taller, and your features changed little by little to conform to your growing body. But what does this have to do with Psalm 139:13-14? It has everything to do with it and I will tell you why.

Let's go back to that moment when you were just a few cells old. How did the cells know to replicate and start forming the different parts of your body? The answer lies in a little thing called DNA.

DNA looks like a spiraling ladder that lives deep inside the cell. It is the map that cells read so they know how to form a body the same way an architect may look at a blueprint to know how to construct a building. From the DNA, the cells will know if they should form to give you light skin, dark skin, blue eyes, or brown eyes, or make you short or tall. Every instruction on how your body will form and how it will look is in the DNA.

Figure 2 is a simplistic drawing of what DNA looks like. Doesn't it look like something that God carefully knit together?

I thought so!

Figure 2

So, when you read in Psalm 139:13 that God formed your inward parts and knitted you together, He did so by knitting together a wonderful sequence, DNA, that made you, You! But it gets better than that!

Psalm 139:14 says that you are wonderfully made, but there is something special about the word "wonderfully."

The original Bible was written in a different language in a series of scrolls. In the case of Psalm 139, it was originally written in Hebrew. Very smart people used those scrolls (or manuscripts) to translate them into English. When they were translating them, they couldn't always include the full meaning of every word. It would make the Bible 10 times longer than it already is!!! So, they had to choose the best word and that is what they did with "wonderfully." But I want to let you in on a little secret. There is a much bigger and more important meaning to the word "wonderfully."

The Hebrew word behind "wonderfully" sounds like this: "Palah." Yes, it means wonderful but not in the way we may think. It means to be wonderfully distinct, different, set apart. It means that each of us is wonderfully different and unique. There is no one else like you!!

And this brings us back to our discussion on DNA. Did you know that no two people have the exact same DNA? In other words, from looking at DNA and things called genes, scientists believe that no two people are exactly alike. Not even twins. Of course not! Because God made you special!!

QUESTIONS for discussion:

1. How does it make you feel that God made you different from everyone else? That there is no one else like you and that you are unique?
2. Knowing that God carefully made us, how should we respond to Him (HINT: the answer is in Psalm 139:14)?

Craft: A Blueprint

Just like our cells use DNA to know how to construct a body, architects and builders use blueprints to know how to construct a house or building. Today you will make a blueprint for a house.

Tools:

Paper
Colored pencils, crayons, or markers.

Directions:

Think about someone in your life who needs a home. Maybe it is a child your family sponsors in another country or someone that is graduating college. Now think about the home that would be ideal for them. How many bedrooms will it have? How many bathrooms? If they are disabled, maybe they need a ramp to get to the front door.

Now that you know how this house will look, draw a blueprint. A blueprint is usually an overhead image of a house or building. **Figure 3** is an example.

Draw your own and label each room!

Figure 3

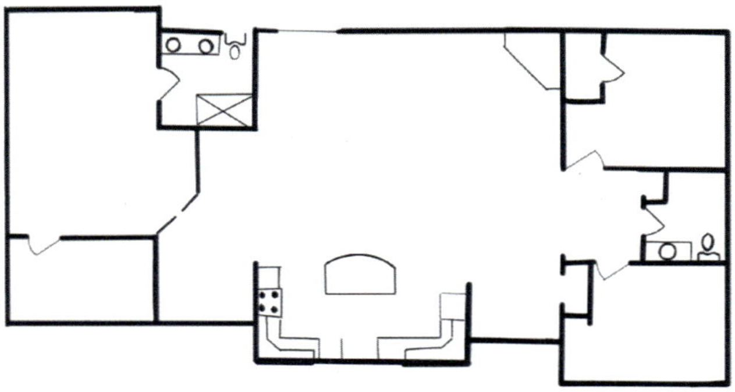

Lesson 3: Be Fruitful and Multiply

In today's lesson, we will go back to Genesis.

Let's read.

> [27] So God created man in his own image, in the image of God he created him; male and female he created them. [28] And God blessed them. And God said to them, "Be fruitful and multiply and fill the earth and subdue it, and have dominion over the fish of the sea and over the birds of the heavens and over every living thing that moves on the earth."
>
> **Genesis 1:27-28 (ESV)**

Verse 27 should now be familiar to you as it is the verse we studied in our first lesson.

What is God's instruction in verse 28?

Right after telling us that He created us in His image, He gives us instructions to be fruitful and multiply.

What do you think that means?

It means that God wanted married couples to have babies, form a family, and then for those babies to grow up into adults, get married, and have more babies.

When God gives us instructions to do something, He also equips us to be able to do it. For example, God wants us to study His Word so he gave us an organ called a brain so that we could read and understand the Bible. For men and women to be fruitful and multiply, He gave them reproductive organs, the parts of the body that help form and nourish a baby.

What do you think would happen if Adam and Eve didn't have reproductive organs?

They would not have been able to have children. Without children, there are no people. For people to multiply, it is necessary for men and women to biologically be able to have children. "Biologically" may be a big word for some of you but it only means that your own bodies are able to form and deliver a child.

But is that the only way to form a family?

No! Some families are formed through adoption. This is important to know because not every woman will be able to have a child biologically. That means that their bodies cannot physically form a baby and so they may adopt instead. Adoption is a wonderful way to form a family because many children around the world don't have parents to care for them and they need moms and dads to adopt them.

There may be other reasons why a woman may not have a child as she follows God's plan for her life. The lesson here is that being able to physically reproduce a child does not make you a girl or a woman. You are a daughter of the King for a very simple reason, He made you a daughter—and that is good enough. But let's now learn more about the reproductive organs because they hold the key to why and how your bodies will change very soon!

Woman's Reproductive Organs:

Reproductive organs are the reason our bodies begin to go through a thing called puberty. It is a time in the life of a girl when her body begins to change rapidly to prepare her reproductive organs for what they were meant to do: form and nourish a baby.

Figure 4 on the next page shows the location of the reproductive organs in a woman.

Figure 4

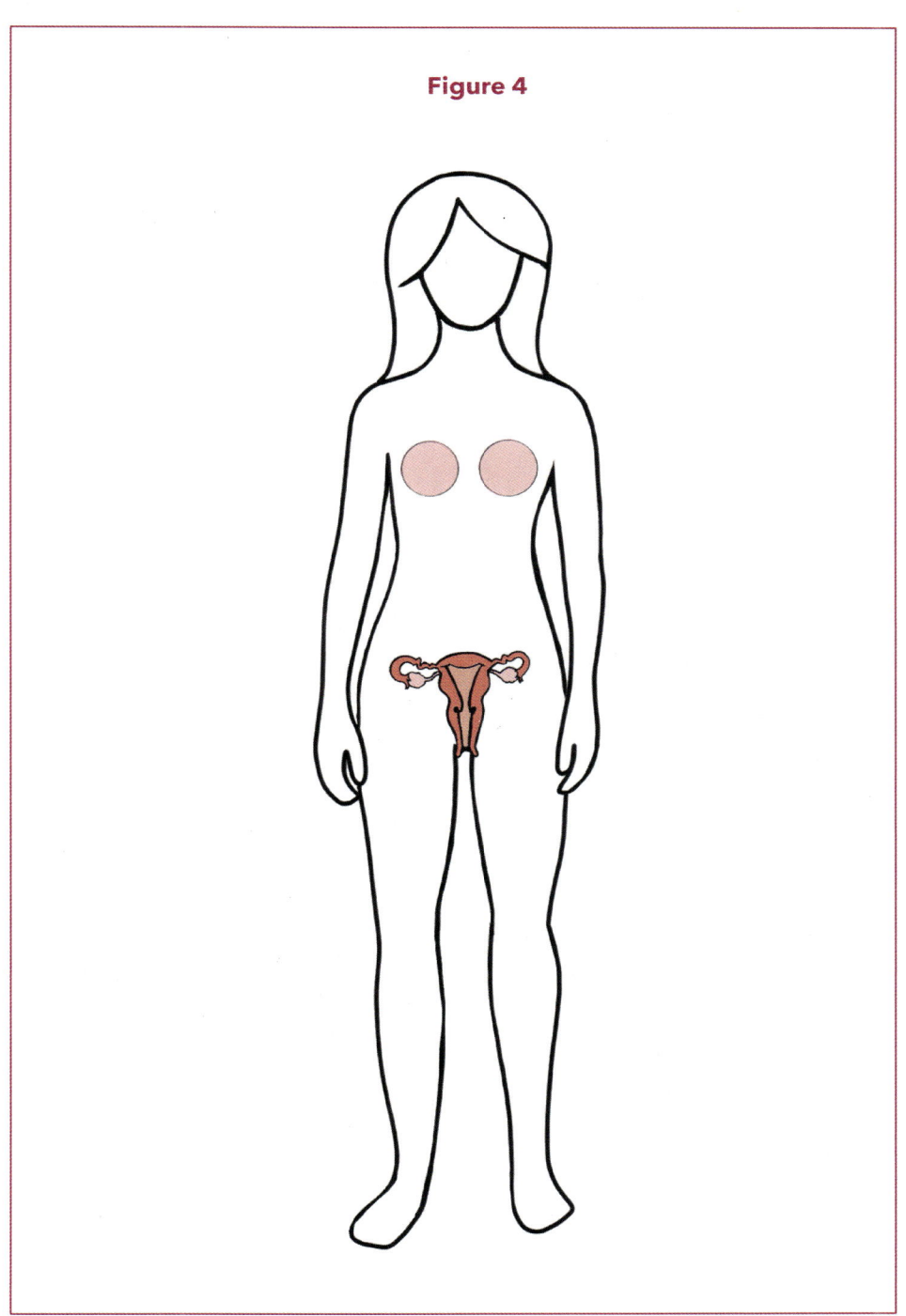

Figure 5 is a close-up image of the lower part of the reproductive system in women.

Figure 5

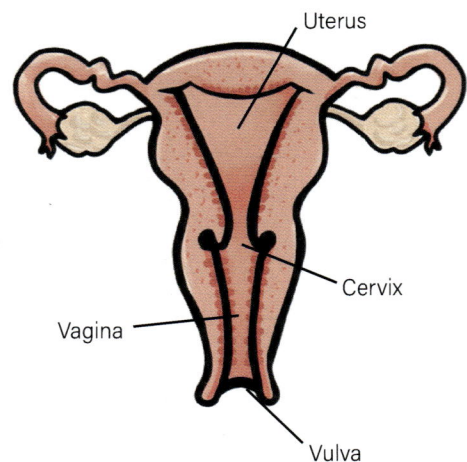

A woman's reproductive organs are made up of quite a few parts. In this lesson, we will learn about the uterus, the cervix, the vagina, the vulva, and the breasts.

The uterus is the part that holds and protects a baby as it grows, and it is also called the womb. When it is time for a baby to be born, it will travel from the uterus to the cervix and come out of the vagina. The vulva is the part outside of the body that connects to the vagina. It is the part you clean when you go to the bathroom, for example. The vulva is also made up of different parts, one of which is called the labia. These are the folds that you may see when washing.

The breasts are especially important after the baby is born. They were designed by God to produce milk so that mothers could feed their babies.

Why do you need to know all of this? Because soon your bodies will begin changing dramatically. You will look different and may even feel different and it is all connected to the reproductive organs. We will explore these changes next week.

Questions for discussion:

1. What are some other commands that God has given you and how has equipped you to carry them out?
2. Can we still be fruitful and multiply as God commanded even though not all women will be able to biologically have kids?
3. What do you enjoy most about being a girl?

Craft: Planting a Seed

God created all animals and vegetation with the ability to multiply. Let's discover how God does that with plants. Did you know that a bean is a seed? Today we will put that theory to the test and plant a bean.

Tools:

Acrylic paints and a brush (optional)
Small glass container (baby food jar works)
A Bean
Cotton Balls

Directions:

Paint the container to your liking. Make sure to leave a little window so you can see your seed grow. Place the cotton balls in the bottom of the jar. Fill the glass with water until the cotton ball is damp but not soaked. Place the bean on the cotton ball. For the next few days, watch it grow! Make sure to keep adding water so the cotton ball remains damp.

Lesson 4: Your Changing Body

In the last lesson, we discovered that God designed reproductive organs so that our bodies could be fruitful and multiply. It is not our bodies' only purpose, but it is an important part of God's design. Those organs are asleep for the first 8 to 13 years of life. But then, one day those sleepy organs begin to wake up. We call this puberty, and it is the beginning of a girl's transformation into womanhood.

Let's read this verse together.

> When I was a child, I spake as a child, I understood as a child, I thought as a child: but when I became a man, I put away childish things.
>
> **I Corinthians 13:11 (ESV)**

Being a child is a beautiful thing! Jesus loved the little children, and he taught us how very precious kids are. But the time comes when all of us must leave the child behind and mature into an adult. Puberty is part of that process, and it pushes our bodies into adulthood. However, it is only a part of what makes an adult an adult. Gaining knowledge and wisdom are also part of maturing. And that is why we are doing this study together so that you will grow in knowledge about your bodies!

Even though we try to learn and become more mature in our minds, we don't have to do anything to help our bodies grow. God, in His wisdom, set our bodies on autopilot so that in the future, our bodies would be ready for adulthood.

If our reproductive organs are asleep, then chemicals called hormones is the thing that wakes them up. Hormones work hard to get all the parts of the reproductive organs working correctly and help them finish growing. For example, a hormone called estrogen causes the breasts to grow.

The hormones also cause our bodies to change in ways that may make us feel uncomfortable. It is important to know what those changes are, so we are not surprised (or worried) when it happens.

Have you seen an older sister or cousin experience puberty? What are some changes that you noticed?

Let's talk about these changes.

Breasts: One of the first signs that you are entering puberty is the development of breast buds (little mounds underneath the nipple). The nipple area may get wider and darker and then the breasts will continue to grow. During this process, your breasts may feel sore or even itchy. This is a good time to go bra shopping because it can help reduce the soreness!! Your mom, grandma, or aunt can help you find the perfect one.

Increase in Hair Growth: You might see more hair growth on your legs and/or arms and you will experience hair growth under your armpits. You will also notice hair growth around the labia (the folds of the skin surrounding the vagina). This is normal.

Physical Changes: You may experience growth spurts. That shirt you loved so much may all of a sudden be too small!

Weight Gain: Weight gain during puberty is normal. Girls can gain up to 15 – 20 lbs. and that is okay. With all the negative talk about being "fat," you may think that "fat" is a bad thing. But actually, the body needs a certain amount of fat to be healthy. The body uses that fat to protect vital organs and even as a source of energy for growth spurts.

It is possible for your body to store too much fat (which can negatively affect things like your heart and joints), but as long as you are eating well-rounded meals with lots of fruits and veggies and not too many sugary snacks, it is not something you need to worry about. However, do know that it is completely normal for extra fat to form around girls' bellies, hips, and buttocks area during puberty. That is a good thing.

Oily Skin: You may experience an increase in oily skin which can lead to pimples. That is a normal part of puberty and some girls have more than others. There are ways to help limit the oil on your skin and control the pimples. Your mom or another trusted adult can help you find the right creams to help keep your skin clean.

Sweating: You might find that you are sweating more and more (in combination with chemical changes in our bodies due to hormones) means that you might produce body odor. Yes, you will be stinkier now when you exercise or even just go about your day. Showers will become more important than ever!

Mood Changes: Hormones help our reproductive organs to develop, but they have an interesting side effect. They can cause sudden moods to change. That means that one moment you could be happy and then unexpectedly, you will get cranky. These are good times to bring our minds back to Jesus to help control our moods!

There is one last change that will be the most dramatic of all! We will go into detail about what that is during our next lesson.

QUESTIONS for discussion:

1. As we have learned, your bodies are still growing, but what are some ways you can also grow in knowledge and wisdom?
2. Is there anything about puberty that worries you? Do you have questions about any of the changes?

Craft: Metamorphosis

We are not the only ones in creation who experience dramatic changes. Many animals and insects also change as they mature. One of the coolest is the transformation of a caterpillar into a butterfly. Today we will make our own caterpillar and butterfly.

Tools:

Clothes Pin
Googly eyes (optional)
Crayons, colored pencils, or paints
Glue
Butterfly wings (Photocopy and cut out Craft Resource A)

Directions:

You will transform your clothespin into a caterpillar. Paint or color the clothespin with crayons, colored pencils, or paints. Glue the googly eyes on top. Your caterpillar is now ready to transform into a butterfly. Cut out the butterfly wings and decorate them. You turn your caterpillar into a butterfly by gluing them to the back of the clothespin.

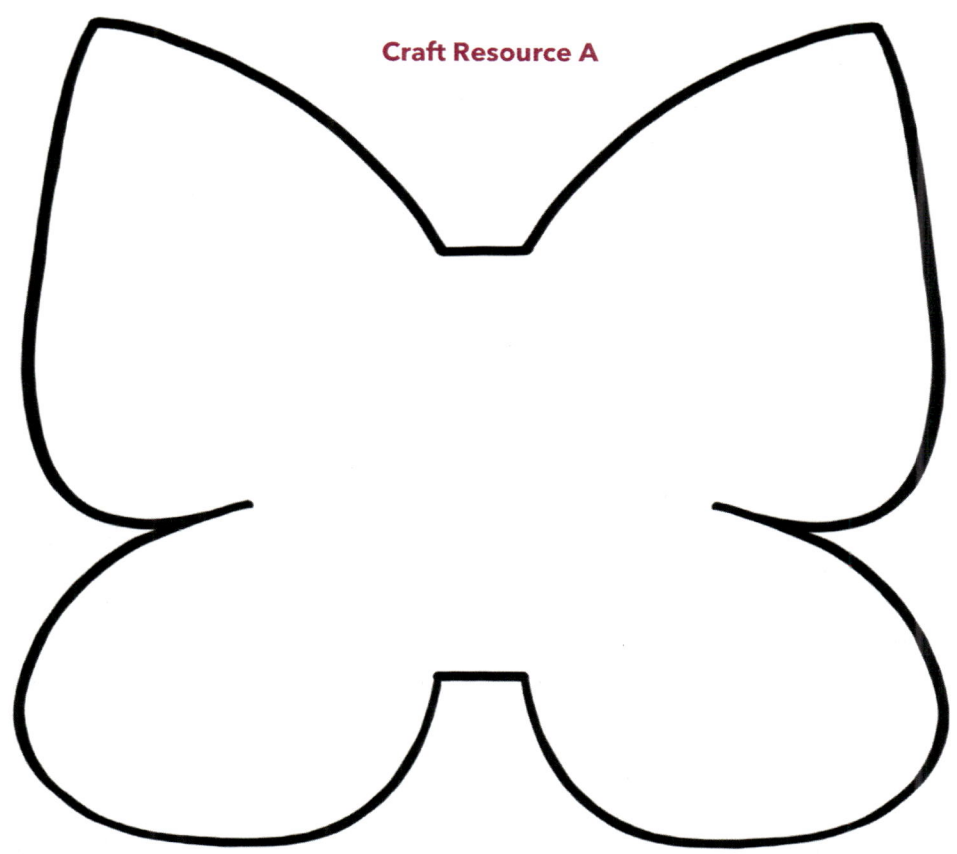

Craft Resource A

Lesson 5: Menstruation

Tools recommended for today's lesson to help with the lesson's discussion:

- *Menstrual Pad*
- *Tampon*

In the last lesson, we learned that once girls begin puberty, their bodies begin to change in a lot of ways.

Can you remember what are some of those ways?

There is one important change that we did not discuss and that is the beginning of the menstrual cycle. This one requires a lesson all of its own so let's get right to it!

The most significant change that girls will experience, about 18 months after the first signs of puberty, is the start of the menstrual cycle. You might have heard it referred to as a period. When girls or women menstruate, blood will be released from the vagina about once a month. The first time you see it, it can feel scary but know that it is completely normal. You are probably wondering, why is there blood? Let's find out.

The menstrual cycle usually lasts about 28 days. Don't panic! The bleeding part only lasts for a few days, but a lot is happening within the uterus during the 28 days. In the first part of the cycle, the hormone called estrogen rises, causing the lining of the uterus to thicken. If a woman was to get pregnant, the lining would nourish the baby. However, when there is no pregnancy, the thicker lining in the uterus is shed through the vagina —— and that is what we call a period. (See **Figure 6**)

Figure 6

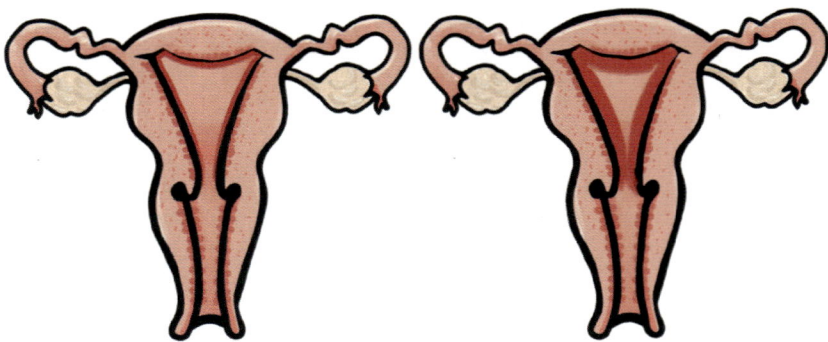

Does it hurt? Some girls and women experience cramps in the area below the belly button and tenderness in the breasts. It can be worse for some than others. If it is too painful, your mom or guardian will help you find ways to ease the pain such as a heating pad or pain relievers.

I know, pain and blood once a month for the next forty or so years does not sound like fun, and you may be wondering why God would have designed it this way. God's intention was not for us to suffer or experience pain like this. But a long time ago, Adam and Eve rebelled against God and the result was a world that was corrupted.

Do you remember what happened?

The serpent deceived Eve and she took the one fruit that God had forbidden. She then gave it to her husband who freely ate from it. Their disobedience resulted in grave consequences. Let's look at Genesis 6 to see what God said to the woman.

> I will surely multiply your pain in childbearing; in pain you shall bring forth children.
>
> **Genesis 3:16A (ESV)**

So, for the woman, part of the consequences of sin entering the world was pain during childbirth. The pain and discomfort girls and women feel when they get their periods are connected to what happened thousands of years ago in the garden of Eden. The menstrual cycle is the body's way of getting ready to form a baby and eventually deliver it. If a baby doesn't come, the body gets rid of the extra stuff, hence a period.

Be not discouraged! Let's find out why in Romans 8:22-24.

> [22] For we know that the whole creation has been groaning together in the pains of childbirth until now. [23] And not only the creation, but we ourselves, who have the firstfruits of the Spirit, groan inwardly as we wait eagerly for adoption as sons, the redemption of our bodies. [24] For in this hope we were saved. Now hope that is seen is not hope. For who hopes for what he sees?
>
> **Romans 8:22-24 (ESV)**

What is Romans saying here? Yes, there is a lot of pain and discomfort that comes with living in a world that has been corrupted. All of creation feels it. There are times when there is pain, suffering, and discomfort, but one day our bodies will be redeemed! Because of Jesus' sacrifice, one day we will have new bodies that feel no pain or discomfort. We rejoice in the hope of what awaits us!

But what about while we are here in a sinful world? The discomfort you may feel as your bodies change will not always be pleasant but remember that God designed those changes to spur you into womanhood. This is the process of leaving childish things behind and maturing into the woman that God made you to be!

And also, remember that our God is gracious, and He has given us the gift of modern medicine. So, whether in childbirth or during our periods, many times there are options to reduce the pain or take it away altogether. In other words, don't be anxious about it!

How to Manage a Menstrual Period

Getting your period can be messy, but thankfully today there are ways to keep the mess to a minimum. To manage a period there are two items women usually use, a **pad** or a **tampon**.

A **pad** comes in different shapes and sizes, and it is placed on your underwear to help absorb the blood. Once the paper on the bottom of the pad is peeled off, it can stick to your underwear to limit shifting. Pads can be very thick, but they can also be very thin. They can cover a large part of your underwear or cover just a little. With time you will find which one works for you. You will, however, need to change these frequently throughout the day.

A **tampon** is usually not for younger girls, but you must know what they are because some of your friends may use them. A tampon is a small cylinder that looks like a rolled-up cotton ball. A tampon usually comes with a plastic applicator. Using the plastic applicator, the tampon is inserted into the vagina to help stop and absorb the flow of blood.

I know what you are thinking. Why would anyone ever want to wear one of those? Some girls and women find them useful if they are at the beach or a water park, for example, because you can't go swimming with a pad on. They are not for everyone, and some girls and women choose not to swim at all when they have their periods. That is okay too!

Remember, menstrual periods start about 18 months after the start of puberty. So, if you don't have breast buds yet, you don't have to worry about a period any time soon. But if you know that you are well into puberty, then you might want to be ready. If you get it at school, just politely ask your teacher if you can go to the nurse's office. You may also want to start carrying a pad in your backpack just in case.

That was a lot to cover! And it may feel weird to talk about it, but don't ever feel weird about asking your parents or guardians about your changing body. The more you know, the better prepared you will be!

QUESTIONS for Discussion?

1. What are your concerns about getting your period?
2. What do you think is the greatest benefit of having your period? (hint: ask your mom)

Craft: Woman Mosaic

The purpose of this craft is to help you think about what it means to grow into womanhood beyond the physical changes to your bodies.

Tools:

Woman Mosaic (Photocopy and cut out **Craft Resource B**)

Directions:

Write words in each space to represent the woman you would like to grow up to be. Possible words or phrases: "loves God," "knowledge," "wisdom," "not prideful," "humble," "capable leader," "knows her Bible," "prayer warrior," "loves people," "responsible," "does not lie," "intelligent." When you are done writing your words, color each block with a different color.

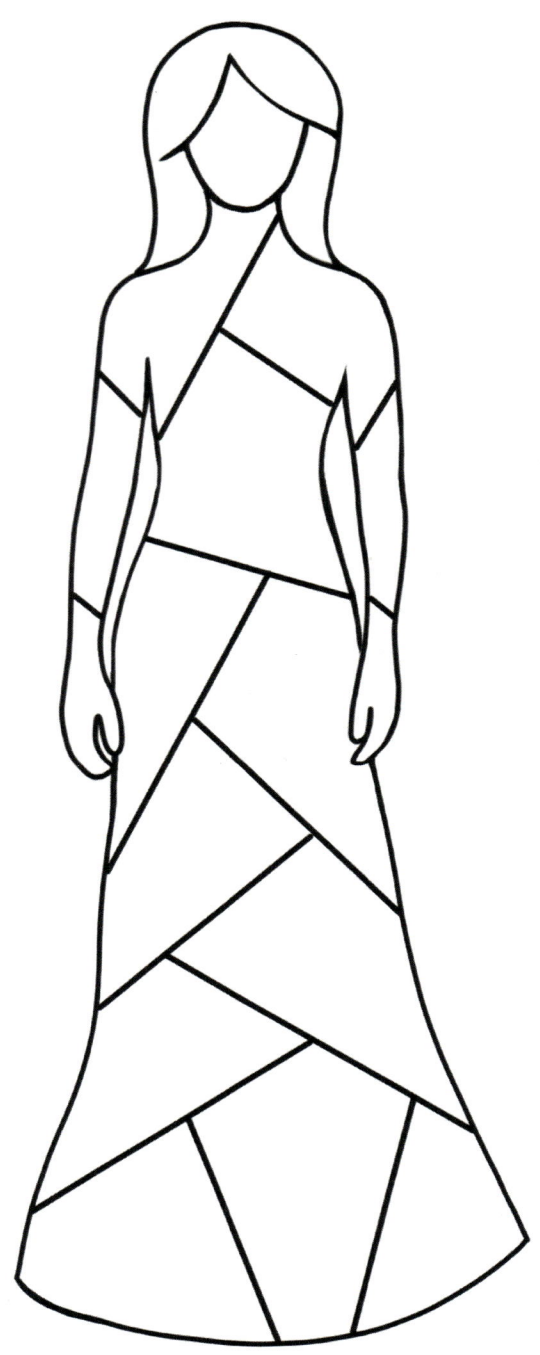

Lesson 6: Becoming One Flesh

In Lesson 3, we learned that God told His creation to be fruitful and multiply. It isn't just people who can multiply, but animals and vegetation as well. If you made the craft from that lesson, by now, your bean will have sprouted and is growing!

Have you ever wondered how babies sprout? You know they grow in their mama's bellies, but how does that process start? One day, do they just spontaneously start growing? Actually, no. To understand how this little miracle happens, we must go back to our image of the uterus (**Figure 7**).

Figure 7

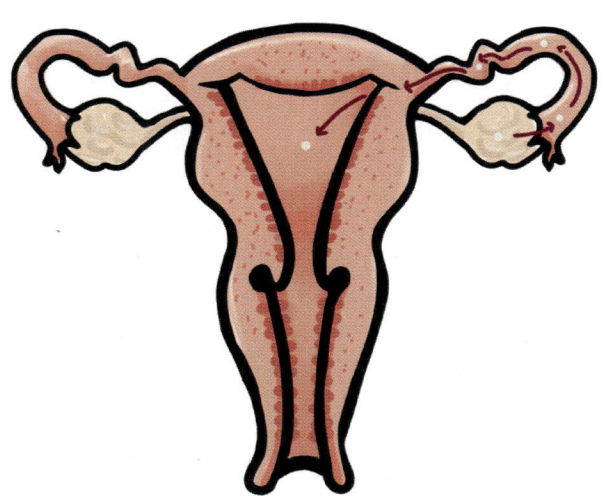

On each side of the uterus, you will see little sacks that contain itty, bitty eggs. Each girl is born with a set number of eggs. During the menstruation cycle, the body releases an egg from the sack, and it travels to the uterus. There, it patiently waits to be fertilized. A fertilized egg will develop into a baby. If it isn't fertilized, then the body will begin shedding the lining (that is your period) and the process starts all over again.

What is fertilization? In people, fertilization happens when a sperm enters the egg. Well, where does the sperm come from? Sperm are found in the reproductive organs of boys and men. Wait, what!?!? I know what you are thinking. We will cover how sperm makes its way into a woman's uterus, but first, we must learn about a boy's reproductive organs.

Figure 8

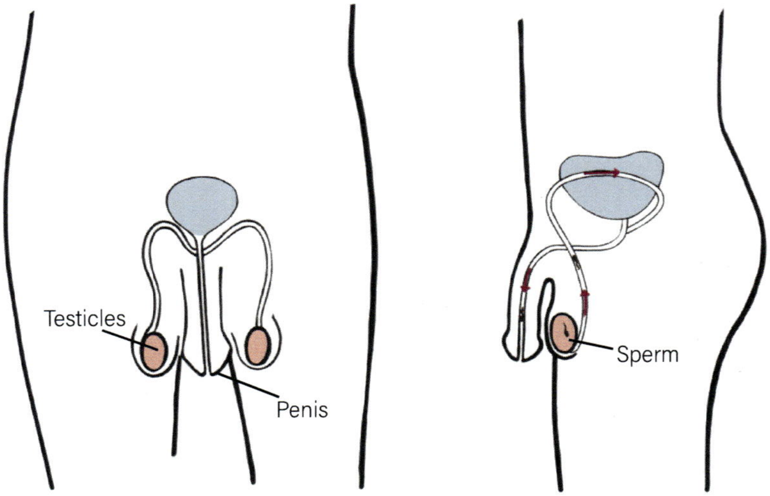

In **Figure 8**, you see that men have testicles and a penis. Testicles hold the sperm and during a thing called sex, the sperm will travel from the testicles and through the penis and be released into a woman's vagina.

What is Sex?

Sex was designed by God to be enjoyed by a husband and wife in a marriage. Let's read more about it in God's word.

> He answered, 'Have you not read that he who created them from the beginning made them male and female, and said, "Therefore a man shall leave his father and his mother and hold fast to his wife, and the two shall become one flesh'? So they are no longer two but one flesh. What therefore God has joined together, let not man separate."
>
> **Matthew 19:4-6 (ESV)**

Sex is when a married man and woman come close together and become one flesh. How do they do that? The husband and wife will hold each other tight and when the wife says it is okay, the husband will insert his penis into her vagina. The sperm will then travel from his testicles, through his penis, into her vagina, and eventually her uterus. In the uterus, if God wills it, the sperm will enter the egg, fertilize it, and a baby will begin to form. It is a beautiful act of love designed by God and meant to be pleasurable for the husband and the wife.

Sex is a beautiful gift, but it can also be dangerous. For example, sex can be painful for a woman. A man that is willing to love a woman the way Jesus loved the church and marry her will take the proper care to become one with his wife in a way that is pleasurable and comfortable and not painful.

Sex can also transmit very serious diseases or make a young girl pregnant before she is mature enough to endure the pain of childbirth and take care of a baby. For this reason, God set very important rules for sex. Let's read.

> [3] For this is the will of God, your sanctification: that you abstain from sexual immorality; [4] that each one of you knows how to control his own body in holiness and honor.
>
> **I Thessalonians 4:3-4 (ESV)**

Sexual immorality is having sex with anyone that is not your husband. It also includes letting people touch your private areas who are not your husband. There are exceptions to the touching rule, like a doctor or nurse during a medical exam. Your parents can help give you other examples of what is okay or not okay.

Remember that you are created in God's image and a masterpiece made by the greatest artist that ever lived. God set rules in place to protect the beauty of His creation. To protect you!

It is always okay to have questions about sex. God created it and He talks a lot about it in the Bible! Some of your friends may think they know a lot about what it is, and you may be tempted to ask them about it. I will lovingly tell you; they will give you bad advice. Remember, no one knows more about sex than your parents. That is how you came into the world after all! So, if you are curious or have questions, ask your parents!

QUESTIONS for Discussion:

1. What are other rules that God has made to protect his people?
2. Does it make sense why God has strict rules about sex?
3. Do you have any other questions about it?

Craft: Family Tree

Sex is the tool God made to create families. So, in today's craft, we will make a family tree! A family tree is a visual representation of a family's history. Usually, you start with the current generation (that is you), and work backwards to your parents, grandparents, and so forth. Go ahead, give it a try!

Tools:

Crayons, colored pencils, or markers
Family Tree Page (Photocopy and cut **Craft Resource C**)

Directions:

Write the names of your family in your family tree. Now color it!

Grandpa | Grandma | Grandpa | Grandma

Dad | Mom

You

Lesson 7: Be the Temple

During these last few lessons, we have learned a lot about how a girl's body changes when she enters puberty. You are gaining knowledge, but as you gain knowledge, you must also gain wisdom. What is wisdom?

Wisdom is being able to make good decisions with the knowledge that we have. You have now learned the different ways your body will change, so now what do you do with that knowledge? Thankfully, scripture, once again, is a good place to start.

Let's read I Corinthians 6:19-20:

[19] Or do you not know that your body is a temple of the Holy Spirit within you, whom you have from God? You are not your own, [20] for you were bought with a price. So glorify God in your body.

I Corinthians 6:19-20 (ESV)

This Bible verse tells us that our body is the temple of the Holy Spirit and that we must glorify God in our bodies.

Imagine you found out Jesus was going to join you for dinner. Would you sit at the table without brushing your teeth, your hair as messy as when you just woke up, and not having showered for a week? Of course not! You would clean up in your Sunday best!

I Corinthians is telling us the Holy Spirit is with us all the time and so we should try to take care of our bodies the best we can. This doesn't mean that the days of playing in the dirt are over. It just means that you must take extra care to keep clean after strenuous activity and always remember to glorify God even in your body.

We have already looked at how to keep our bodies clean during menstruation in a previous lesson. Now let's look at some other examples.

Body Odor: Remember, that more sweating and an increase in body odor are normal changes you will experience when entering puberty. That means that you will have to take extra care to keep your body clean. You will probably have to shower more frequently, for starters, and when you are ready, you might have to start wearing deodorant. If you don't know what that is, deodorant is a substance you put under your armpits to help limit sweating and bad odors.

Increased Hair Growth: You may have heard or seen someone shave their legs or armpits. Shaving is a way many women like to keep themselves groomed. Your parents may want you to hold off shaving as long as possible, so talk to your parents or guardian first. They will help you decide when it is a good time if at all. Whatever you do, don't shave without an adult's help!! Don't shave your arms and never, ever shave your face!

Oily Skin: Remember how we talked about an increase in oily skin, and how you may start to see pimples? Practicing good skincare is an important activity to start young and not just to avoid pimples. Good skincare habits can help avoid damage to your skin from the sun, for example. It can be as simple as just washing your face in the morning when you wake up, in the evening before you go to bed, and adding a little bit of cream with sunscreen. Your parent or guardian can help you decide on the best skincare practice for your age. Remember, that what your mom may use for her face may not be the best for you and may be harmful for your skin. Always talk to your parents or guardians before putting anything new on your skin.

Nutrition: Good nutrition is always important. Foods like fruits, vegetables, and yogurt can keep your body working properly. It can help you ward off illnesses, help you be more alert when you are studying, and keep your organs functioning at top capacity. Good nutrition should always be about making sure your body is staying healthy and that you are taking good care of the body God gave you to glorify Him. It is not really about looks. Excess weight can adversely affect your joints or how your heart pumps blood. However, someone can be very thin, and still be making bad nutritional choices that can affect their health. Your doctor and parents or guardian can help you decide what is the best combination of foods for you!

Remember, the women in your life that you trust (your mom, aunt, Sunday school teacher, etc.) have already gone through this. You don't have to go through puberty alone! They know a lot, a lot more than your friends. Let them help you navigate all these changes. Always ask them first because your friends may not give you the right answers!

QUESTIONS for Discussion:

1. What are some ways that you can glorify God in the way you eat?
2. What are some ways you can glorify God in the way you dress?
3. What are some questions you have about taking care of your body?

Craft: Make Your Own Perfume

Perfume is one way to help keep your body smelling good as you enter puberty. However, sometimes the perfumes used by adults can be too strong for young girls. Today, you get to make a perfume that is right for you.

Tools:

(Note to parents: Your essential oil-loving friends will be able to help you find the best places to get these items. They may even lend you a few essential oils for this craft. You only need a few drops.)

Little amber glass bottles
Essential oils (lavender, sweet orange, jasmine, and vanilla are good options)
A carrier oil (jojoba oil)

Directions:

Fill the glass bottles with the carrier oil. Pick an essential oil or two that you like. Pour only 1 or 2 drops of each oil into your bottle. Shake it up and try out your new perfume!

Lesson 8: Bearing His Image

Girls, I hope you are feeling smarter. I know I am with everything we have learned about our bodies! We learned that we are created in God's image and that God carefully and wonderfully made us unique. We also learned that our bodies were designed with reproductive organs that launch girls into puberty and eventually womanhood! But we've also learned that as our bodies change, our minds must mature along with it. We must grow in knowledge and in wisdom and make good choices that glorify God. This is called bearing God's image.

It is in Genesis 1:27 that we learned that we were created in God's image. But when sin entered the world, a few chapters later in Genesis, that image was marred. It was as if someone threw a bucket of mud on that beautiful Picasso painting. It didn't decrease the value of the painting because a Picasso is still a Picasso, but it made it hard for others to see that it truly was a work of art made by a glorious God. The art dealers couldn't recognize that it was priceless. They wanted to throw that masterpiece away, but Jesus said, "Hold on! My Father, the artist, wants His masterpiece back and I will give my life in exchange for it."

Yes, Jesus bought us back. He paid the ultimate price to return that muddied, marred work of art back to its Creator. So what are we to do? How do we begin the process of cleaning ourselves off from all the grime and reflect the artistry of our Creator?

> [8] But now you must put them all away: anger, wrath, malice, slander, and obscene talk from your mouth. [9] Do not lie to one another, seeing that you have put off the old self with its practices [10] and have put on the new self, which is being renewed in knowledge after the image of its creator.
>
> **Colossians 3:8-10 (ESV)**

In this verse in Colossians, God is asking us to put away sin and behaviors that do not reflect the character of Jesus. Even though a girl's body is on autopilot and her body will change her into a woman, that is only part of the process. The second part requires us to do our part. As our body sheds its childhood, our minds must also shed its childhood to become women of God that reflect Jesus.

> Just as we have borne the image of the man of dust, we shall also bear the image of the man of heaven.
>
> **I Corinthians 15:49 (ESV)**

The man of heaven in this verse is talking about Jesus. We must bear the image of Jesus who is the perfect image of God. We must try to be more like Jesus in the things we do and that is how we begin to clean the mud off.

The first step in reflecting the image of God begins with one word. Circle the word knowledge in Colossians 3:9-10 (on the previous page). Our image, our self, God's masterpiece is renewed in knowledge.

What kind of knowledge do you think you need?

Yes! Knowledge of God's word. Your transformation into womanhood begins with knowing your Bible. The more you know the scriptures, the more you will know the heart of God. So, let's begin the process of polishing this wonderful work of art that God made us. Let's start scrubbing off all that mud and that begins by becoming girls and eventually women who know the Word of God!!

I leave you with one verse to reflect on as we finish this study:

> For we are his workmanship, created in Christ Jesus for good works, which God prepared beforehand, that we should walk in them.
>
> **Ephesians 2:10 (ESV)**

QUESTIONS for Discussion:

1. What are some things you can do to learn God's word?
2. What are sins in your life that you can "put away"?
3. What are some ways you can reflect the heart of Jesus?

Craft: Masterpiece Bookmark

Part of bearing God's image means knowing His word. To help launch you into the process of becoming a woman of the word, we are going to create a bookmark. You can use this bookmark as you study your Bible, so you do not lose your place!!!!

Tools:

Colored pencils, crayons, or markers.
Bookmark (Photocopy and cut out **Craft Resource D**)
Scissors

Directions:

Cut out the bookmarks. You can either color the bookmark provided for "His Masterpiece" or you can make your own. Or you can do both!

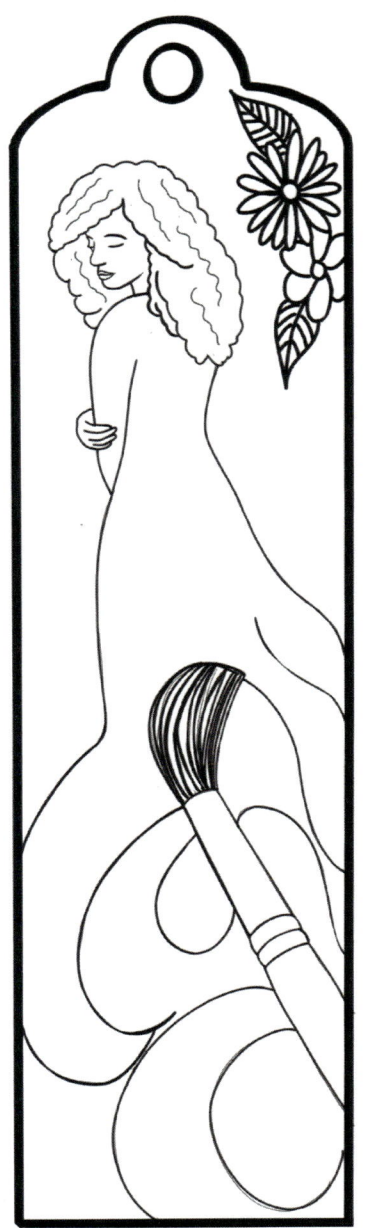

More from Luisa Rodriguez

Book

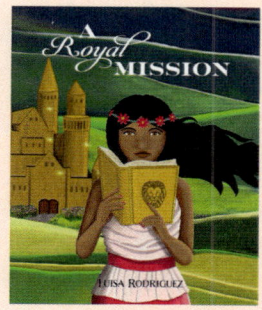

A Royal Mission

A Children's Book for Girls

Through striking illustrations and a captivating plot, girls learn about their God-given purpose, how much they are loved, and what it means to serve the King.

8 x 10 Lined Notebooks

6 x 9 Prayer, Sermon, and Lined Notebooks

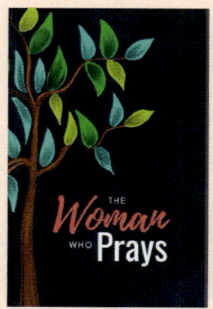

Discover more at FruitfullyWrite.com

Made in the USA
Coppell, TX
05 July 2025

51511649R00029